Broken Blossoms

Maryann Hurtt's *Broken Blossoms* knows that the bloom, in a temporal world, is always fleeting but that the perfume of the flower—that sacred and kind metaphor for what it means to be human, vulnerable and beautiful—is inexhaustible and eternal through the gift of memory, observation, epiphany, and even suffering. Hurtt's poems are the work of a caregiver, a nurturer, a poet that sees in the world those same offerings of care and attentiveness brought to the senses in the common scenes of everyday life. These poems find beauty where others may not seek nor dare to look; Hurtt clearly knows that beauty, kindness, power, and wisdom are often the fruits, not of perfect and fragrant things but of broken and overlooked things whose true perfume can only be extracted by the deft hand of one who is accustomed to finding loveliness in the splendor of those things others do not notice nor take heed of.

—Aaron Abeyta
author of *colcha*,
former Poet Laureate of Colorado's Western Slope

Maryann Hurtt's new book, *Broken Blossoms*, wonders at, insists on, is in awe of, and embraces this paradox at its heart: "knowing we carry on / even as we ghost away." Pervasive and intimate, this experience connects speakers in the poems to other people and to larger than human nature. It is an active process, shown in powerful active verbs: "sumac screams red," a favorite tree "scudded leaves," and in war an officer "mother-birded mush" to a child. The poems blossom with transformed life. 1960s love beads become flower seeds, dead fish become roses, and a mother's anger that "purpled the room" passes into "air now sweet and clear enough / to stitch your heart pieces / whole again." This flow between pain and joy, life and death, is signaled by an absence of terminal punctuation. Hurtt's poems become acts of faith that life, even at its end, is "still full of promise."

—Margaret Rozga
author of *Holding My Selves Together*,
Wisconsin Poet Laureate 2019-2020

Chock full of flowers, lyrical language, and hand-me-down stories, Maryann Hurtt's *Broken Blossoms* is richly remembered, lovingly imagined, and deeply attentive to the nuances of the natural and human worlds and the magical moments when they collide.

—Joe Wilkins
author of *Fall Back Down When I Die*
and *When We Were Birds*

Don't let the title fool you. *Broken Blossoms* is full of the very vibrant and verdant joys of the natural world. This collection considers the ability to find wholeness from broken bits, solace in grief, and sincere joy in the wondrous blossoms offered to us each day, if only we take the time to notice.

—Laura Pritchett
winner of the PEN USA Award in Fiction

At the boundary of the vivid and the inexplicable, these poems offer to translate enigma into story, then and there into here and now, lost into found. When time has shrunk to a few scant moments, the density of memory needs these poems to seep into song. Plunge into Hurtt's mysteries, where pain and beauty are equally precious, as each needs the other to heal and be whole. The book proves again and again that the broken can still bloom.

—Kim Stafford
author of *As the Sky Begins to Change*,
Oregon Poet Laureate 2018-2020

Hurtt's poems are lyrical and often moving, casting patterns of light and dark, hope and fear. She is a nature poet in the way that Li Bai is a nature poet, finding in nature an endless series of funhouse mirrors reflecting a fleeting image of the self. Beneath these minimalist poems are whole worlds of feelings.

—Benjamin P. Myers
author of *The Family Book*,
Oklahoma Poet Laureate 2015–2016

The poetry I love best holds the quotidian and the spectacular in the same pair of hands and is spacious enough to embrace both sorrow and joy. Nothing is lost in Maryann Hurtt's perceptive gaze. She sees the world as it is and recognizes moments of beauty in the most desperate settings, as in "Love Her Tender This Hard Rain Night," the final two stanzas: "moon and clouds slip / bits of light / and you see a couple / hovered together / their hands stroking warmth / to rag-covered legs / sweet intimacy this dark night / and a hard rain / is still going to fall." Hurtt's words are as clear and precise as her vision, and not a word is wasted. Get a copy of *Broken Blossoms* for yourself and another for someone who needs a little tenderness.

—Donna Hilbert
author of *Threnody*

Maryann Hurtt captures the great and stunning shimmer of life. Pain, transcendence, and surprise. *Broken Blossoms* is a tender walk through transformative experience.

—Debra Magpie Earling
author of *Perma Red* and *The Lost Journals of Sacajewea*

In *Broken Blossoms*, Maryann Hurtt witnesses in spare, story-telling language the beauty and hurt in our world. In "Purple Orchids and Agent Orange," you find yourself in a Vietnam market where "orchids / so purple, so pink / you believe you have landed / in a rainbow / ...down the hall / a butcher lays out / livers, brains, hearts / ...a young man rolls by... / a foot born in reverse / and only a stump below his knee." Following a mass shooting, a Queen Ann's Lace is surrounded by bright red sumac, and "we all bleed when even / one of us is touched." These poems ask us as readers to witness, too, all the lives and deaths around us.

—Robin Chapman
author of *The Only Home We Know* and *Panic Season*

In *Broken Blossoms*, Maryann Hurtt casts an unflinching eye on "the scald of a world in blazes," asking "who will save us when the sun bursts?" We meet war veterans, Hibakusha, the unhoused, outlaws, and kin—both human and other species—as they succumb to violence, illness, age, and pass on. Yet in these pages, pain and struggle are the neighbors of grace and dignity. In the natural world's "dazzle of dragonflies," "sunflower yellow gem corn," and gator baby's "tiny heartbeat," Hurtt finds the healing balm, the connection, and the knowledge that "we carry on / even as we ghost away" and gifts it to us in striking images that only the most observant of poets can conjure.

—Brenda Cárdenas
author of *Trace*,
Wisconsin Poet Laureate

Maryann Hurtt's *Broken Blossoms* is a lively bouquet of sense and place. As comfortable in the vase of the reader's hands as growing wild. Turn your world purple and pick up a copy.

—Cameron Scott
author of *Watershed*

Broken Blossoms

Maryann Hurtt

Fernwood
PRESS

Broken Blossoms
©2025 by Maryann Hurtt

Fernwood Press
Newberg, Oregon
www.fernwoodpress.com

All rights reserved. No part may be reproduced
for any commercial purpose by any method without
permission in writing from the copyright holder.

Printed in the United States of America

Cover and page design: Mareesa Fawver Moss
Cover image: Loie Fuller in Salome costume. Photographer Van Bosch, 1895.
  From the New York Public Library via Unsplash.

ISBN 978-1-59498-190-6

For H D
in good, bad, and ugly times

Contents

Preface 15
Of Peonies and Murderous Doings 16
Even the Queen's Lace 17
Sunflower-Yellow Gem Corn Hoop Dancing 18
Weeds 19
Purple Orchids and Agent Orange 20
Pang Nue Le 21
in April 22
Questions for the Garter Snake in My Backyard 23
Smitten 24
Killing Field 25
Raspberries and Roses 26
Blue-Stemmed Goldenrod Solidago Lessons 27
Old Men and River Salmon 28
Forty Years After the War 29
Bob's Once and Forever Bomb 30
When We Were So Young 31
Uncommon Substance 32
American Hibakusha* 33
Four-Leaf Entitlement 34
Purple-Posey Love 35

Love Her Tender This Hard-Rain Night ... 36
at the new big wong ... 37
Alligator Farm Blues ... 38
Crossing the River at Leesburg ... 39
Horseradish Tears ... 40
How Do I Write about Dazzles and Dragons
   On a Day the World Is On Fire ... 41
These Feathers ... 42
Transubstantiation ... 43
Farm Wife Drowns ... 44
Lady Liberty, Mosquitoes, and Deer Flies ... 45
After the Bloom ... 46
Hired Man Down ... 47
Letters and Petals ... 48
Shape-shifting in Pandemic Time ... 49
Just a Blink ... 50
Loss and Found ... 51
Waiting for Jesus in Tucson ... 52
Braiding His Wife's Hair ... 53
How To Smell Purple ... 54
Madonna Lily ... 55
Love Beads and a Fog Horn ... 56
Father Bird ... 57
Oh, Darling, Stand by Me ... 58
Home Front ... 59
To Know Such Beauty ... 60
Last-Chance Melody ... 61
Unnamed ... 62
My Mother's Temper ... 63
The Weight of Squid on a Full Moon Night ... 64
Saffron Dreams ... 65
Even Dead Fish Become Roses ... 66
Thurston High School, 6 a.m. ... 67

Acknowledgments ... 69
Title Index ... 73
First Line Index ... 77

Solace is the art of asking the beautiful question of
ourselves, of our world or of one another, often in
fiercely difficult and un-beautiful moments.
—David Whyte

I bloomed up all over again despite knowing,
cherry blossoms are only meant to wither.
—Eayra

And even with all the broken pieces we are whole.
—Christina Persika

Preface

I grew up in a family of storytellers. By the time I was twelve, I knew I wanted to be a "storyteller (a good one)"—at least according to my sixth-grade diary. Some things never change. Now retired after thirty years working as a hospice RN with before and after gigs as a cook, library assistant, museum guide, writer, social worker, and bus girl, stories continue to nourish me..

Shortly before my grandpa died, he shared that as a young man he visited Frank James (of the famous James Gang and brother of Jesse) and how Frank grew beautiful peonies. His story and all the stories heard over the years make me want to know, write, and love the meat, broth, and bones. This sense was never so strong as when I watched folks leave this life.

The poems in *Broken Blossoms* struggle with this tension of beauty and pain. I believe in my deepest heart that we are made to pay attention to all the wonder. A way to live in grace and gratitude.

Maryann Hurtt 2022

Of Peonies and Murderous Doings

my grandfather tells a story
how as a young man
he made his way to Clay County
backcountry
Missouri
where Frank James
existed out his last years
after a lifetime
of rebel yelling-robbing
and assorted other murderous doings
but now most remarkable
about old renegade James
was the quarter my grandpa gave
to gawk at his house
and those front-yard peonies
blooming pink-purple
gorgeous
almost like blood gone sweet

Even the Queen's Lace

on this August day the sky
so blue and deep
you believe nothing evil
could ever exist
but your head rewinds
news
over and again

see how the sumac screams red
its seeds send drops of blood
to the Queen
who thought her lace
was pure
but soon will understand
we all bleed when even
one of us is touched

*following the Dayton and El Paso
mass shootings 2019*

Sunflower-Yellow Gem Corn Hoop Dancing

I chop celery, cabbage
potatoes
feel the heat
of *horno*'s first fire
watch the miracle of dough
becoming bread
know in my bones
not in my ears
the blessing of the new domed
adobe oven
listen now
how the drums, the hoop dancers
draw circles
in my waiting heart
and the pale old grandpa
of gone-too-young Tino
hoop dancer extraordinaire
gives me corn
sunflower-yellow gem corn
slips the kernels into an oily old popcorn bag
instructs me
take them back to Wisconsin
plant them in the light
where his grandson will grow
taste the sun
dance again

*horno—mud adobe-built outdoor oven

Weeds

> He is growing like a weed.
> I love weeds.
>
> *T K*

too much pain
when her son left too early
but now the son
of her son
sprouts bigger and bigger
in glorious grandeur
almost like dandelions
the way they break
through concrete
and now the way her heart
feels the sun—
cracks wide open
over and again

Purple Orchids and Agent Orange
Saigon-Ho Chi Minh City 2019

at Ben Thanh Market
a flower stall holds orchids
so purple, so blue, so pink
you believe you have landed
in a rainbow
where everything kind is possible

down the hall
a butcher lays out
livers, brains, hearts

a young man rolls by
his four-wheel, oversized skate board
propelled with splayed
backward hands
a foot born in reverse
and only a stump below his knee

he looks up
smiles
bright as any sun
creator of rainbows

you wonder about forgiveness
the vendor's fish
its forever accusing eyes

Pang Nue Le

at the farmers market
an old man pulls sunflowers, gladiolas
and other flowers
I have no name for
into bouquets
of August summer
a grandson
takes my money
his father spells out *sunflower* in Hmong
I listen to a tune
that needs no language

in April

the house sinks
deeper and deeper
neighbors say dead mice head to tail
lined window sills
they didn't find his body
for too many days

the dogs whined
their empty bowls flipped

today I walk past hip-high weeds
hear echoes
of cursing and howling
the way I heard
early on a morning
when the sun poured honey

my shoulders warm
the light never finding his

and funny how the daffodils
he couldn't see
still rise every April

Questions for the Garter Snake in My Backyard

out behind the lavender patch
a snake skin slides
into invisible
while the queen bee hums wings
in and out of blossoms
that tower above dirt
cradling someone's old life
soon I won't even recognize
evidence of an existence
now transformed

does the bee know
where your new self travels?
do you still smell lavender
wherever you have gone?
is it possible to let go
of everything you have ever known
and swing your hips
to new tunes?

Smitten

my mother was smitten
for fleabane
the tiny daisy but not really a daisy
flower I see on my hike today
it's end-of-July hot
and I wait for sweet berries
listen, all these pieces
do fit together
the way strawberries
the wild ones
picked themselves
into her palm
and the fleabane
made her drop down
to caress their miniature lives
I believe she knew their language
small talk really
but her heart savvy
in the how and why and where

Killing Field

once again
I go to the killing field
and like every spring
find bleached raccoon skulls
lying among purple anemone
their eyeless sockets
stare into the sky
so blue
it almost strikes me
into seeing

I want to know
their lives, their deaths
how beneath my feet
crumpled leaves
will soon be dirt
how it's possible
to come up purple blossom
and how to the east
sandhill cranes honk dinosaur songs
even as we slide from breath
to breathless
and breath all over again

Raspberries and Roses

smell this
you say
hold out petal perfect
circles
tell me you grafted
raspberries and roses
how the thorns still prick
but oh, to taste pink
even when we bleed crimson

Blue-Stemmed Goldenrod
Solidago Lessons

if I cast a spell and say
solidago ten times
will I understand the way green
transforms to gold
and then to dun and at last
learn to love not just glitter
but the calm of dun
the way end-of-October leaves
slip to the ground
become dirt
the way we evolve into something
beyond our old selves
gifting a future
that circles round and round

Old Men and River Salmon

my father is old now
maybe our last hike together
after a lifetime
of huckleberry summers
and river knowledge
we follow a stream to Waldo Lake
salmon bunched up
in glorious red spawning
last hurrah
fervor
I believe he knows this rite
consolation when leaving this life
we give ourselves back
but home again
knowing we carry on
even as we ghost away

Forty Years After the War

you work the graveyard shift
walk down long hallways
empty bedpans
turn old bodies side to side
soothe nightmares
but when the night is too quiet
the dark remembers sirens
smoke and fire
strewn limbs
and the way a person knows
horror not shared
in daylight
and how the whistles blew
your brother's broken leg dragging
the family slowly
to the shelter that would take no more
and how hope is lost
but still you move farther
till at last
squeezed into a faraway shelter
you listen to bombs wail destruction
and wait and wait
for the all-clear siren
then climb steep stairs
and pass the shelter
that did not take you
and witness its direct hit
while you and your family walk home
one more day

Bob's Once and Forever Bomb

my old auntie holds out her hands
the way long-gone
left-too-early husband Bob
showed her
tells me how the sailors were ordered
protect yourself
cover your eyes
but he spread his fingers
opened them wide enough
to see
radiation glow of skeletal claws
chasing him dawn to dusk, day
and forever night

When We Were So Young
A Kodak moment 1960

all my cousins
sitting in a tree
the backyard cherry
our uncle tended so carefully

see how the branches
braced hands and arms
and Michael's disappearing foot

ten years slip by
booze and war send thieves
they steal pieces of you

till now you are gone

and we never held you
close enough

Uncommon Substance

his eyes watch over the old nurse
in a time-stuck
World War II photo
she lies in bed
oxygen tubing now her companion
memories, too
Sicily, France, Africa
the blood of soldiers
forever blended
in her shrinking body
she says she has no regrets
this life of uncommon substance
where the smell of roses
shares equal time with metallic reek
of warm blood
she has known it all
soon she won't be fighting
for another breath
what escapes now
will join the exhalations
of what we give back
when we are done here

American Hibakusha*

sixty years after you walked
streets radiated
to kingdom come
I watch the ruby red
of your never-ending blood
smell Nagasaki reek
and witness life
storm from here to there

who will save us when the sun bursts?

*Hibakusha is a victim of the atomic bombs
that fell on Hiroshima and Nagasaki

Four-Leaf Entitlement

this glorious start of day
full of birdsong
a four-leaf clover picks itself
straight into my hands

down the trail
a creature's bones and tufts of fur
float and sit among
tiny fleabane

only ghost breath now
on a morning
she never got to love

Purple-Posey Love

at thirteen
I took the 3F bus
got off on M Street
then wandered second-hand shops
where secrets lay
in musty pages

I held a book
of Whittier's poems
when posies and a note
slipped into my lap
letters faded but legible
the petals worn but still purple

love from Jonathon
April 29, 1862

today I dream of Jonathon
wonder whose hands clasped
blossoms violet sweet
and how even now
I want to believe
in once-upon-a-true
everlasting
purple-posey love

Love Her Tender This Hard-Rain Night

on Burnside
Portland street where 100 years back
liquor, whores, and sailors
crowded the alleys
you look for the #8 bus and
it's a hard-rain night

but now under storefront stoops
you see bodies curled in
forever-wet bags
their rusty grocery carts full of mystery
only tarp-tattered protection

moon and clouds slip
bits of light
and you see a couple
hovered together
their hands stroking warmth
to rag-covered legs

sweet intimacy this dark night
and a hard rain
is still going to fall

at the new big wong

my friend Ben
orders duck soup
sifts through the broth
finds bone chips
tells me
you know
they can prick your intestines
at least that is what his mother
always told him
then he continues
to sip, pick, chew, and chance
random acts of violence
and understands
to live is to love
this duck soup
meat, broth, and the bones

Alligator Farm Blues

gulf waters cradle dolphins
my mother and me
we share waves

four months back
the water of my body
no longer held the little one
swimming in me
then slipped too far away

we follow *Alligator Farm* signs
murky water hides bodies
when a farm worker hands me
a gator baby
she fits perfectly in my hands
I rock this someday shoe
feel her tiny heartbeat
want to believe life
keeps pulsing

Crossing the River at Leesburg
100 years after the 1861 Battle of Ball's Bluff

when I was twelve
I waded the Potomac
trusting its watery arms
to hold me
still, I felt the pull
of borders
north and south

fifty years slip by
I study war
read history books

young and old terrified
their brothers washed downriver
the war once so glorious
becomes the warmth of blood
drowning dreams
enemy and friend joined
into open then closed eye bond

gray and blue
make no difference
when it's time to say
goodbye

licking Washington's shores
the river ran red

Horseradish Tears

maybe this man
so full of leftover Vietnam blues
can only cry
horseradish tears
he grates their gnarled tubular roots
I wash the jars
he packs them full
tiny pots of sorrow and bite
a way to contain
for this little while
the war that never ends

How Do I Write about Dazzles and Dragons On a Day the World Is On Fire
May 25, 2020

1.
Tripping the Light Fantastic

surrounded by tiny wings
I trot my way through roots and rocks
my feet believe in flight
think I might in another life
become iridescence
but for now
a dazzle of beginnings
is enough this May-day dawn
when our broken world dreams
transformation
and I dance with the dragons

2.
Phoenix

on a day I write
a dazzle of dragonflies
and dream of iridescence
I startle awake to feel
the scald of a world in blazes
hear screams howl
I can't breathe
and know right now
it is time for me
and all my dragon brothers and sisters
to dance in flames and fury
our souls burn in the ashes
ready to fly again

These Feathers

seem innocent
even pure
like nothing hard or bad
ever happened
they lift off the slate-slabbed trail
float their way to the bay
where whitefish think they have found
a new mother or maybe a cousin
I want my leaving
to be this
of course, blood and bones and guts
but in the end
to know
we really are kin

Transubstantiation

on that day
when pewter rains
mark November
and deer run frenzied
chase dream mates
you, in the tire of a too fast car
die

I stare at the puddling
pooling of your now still body
while vultures descend
feed and clean

come December
your ribs stick up and out
the snowy field
like dense harp string
bass notes
the wind laments a dirge

the almost green of spring arrives
wild blue phlox mark
your invisible body
but now you are wings

sky held
ebony specks

Farm Wife Drowns

she always knew
the end would come some day
understood life and death numbers
after all had been a farm wife
for God knows how long
but on a spring day
when green finally colored the land
and cottonwoods blew kisses
there she was chasing geese
when in one wild slip
hit the water
made the leap
from here to there

Lady Liberty, Mosquitoes, and Deer Flies

carry a big stick
he tells me
the deer flies will swarm it
at dusk tonight
I try my version
long-stemmed Queen Ann's lace
held high like
some kind of flower child
lady liberty
I run softly
the Ice Age Trail
where mosquitoes and deer flies
call wetland kettles home
and for this little while
we share this piece of earth

After the Bloom

your wife taught me
to harvest seeds
they sleep over winter
then come spring
we welcome them back
where now on this July day
I know the joy
of orange
and you
your bloom long gone
but still light

Hired Man Down

the hired man lies
in musty sheets and patched quilts
his barn room insulated
from early spring chill
stacks of *National Geographic*
dry hay and greasy tools
sit in corners

the one window
leaks the farm kids' giggles
they tiptoe into his room
rock back and forth

they never knew him to be down

his breaths grow louder
his gut draining away
the air around him fills with odor
so different than
the sweet smell of manure

he knows what to do
the animals taught him well

lie low
breathe in
breathe out
slower and slower

until

Letters and Petals

an almost lifetime ago
I walked past a poppy field
their orange blooms flaunting
themselves in the sun
then three blocks further
to Fifth Street School
where Dick and Jane taught me
to read and write
my fingers gripping a pencil
scribing the curvature
of flowers
the touch of words
their ever-blossoming mystery

Shape-shifting in Pandemic Time

no longer rushing out the door
primed for a day
of responsibility and decorum
we slide into morning
more intent on wood ducks
and daffodils
my friend walks her labyrinth
dressed only in bright bird-red
some might think
it's a robe covering
early spring cold
but she knows better
today she is Giant Cardinal
just moseying along
slipping into a different life
where knowing light
and finding a few seeds
are all that matter

Just a Blink

on crimson-stained snow
morning dove's life
is snatched from winter chill

she flies in cooper hawk's talons

come spring a young hawk
screeches new songs
his mother celebrates their survival

dove carries on
simply new shape

Loss and Found

in November
he eased her to the window
their favorite tree
scudded leaves
till bare

back to the sick bed
her breaths leaked into air
became vapor
then left

in spring
the cherry tree
snowed petals

come August
sweet
then sour
then sweet-sour
everlasting
fruit-luscious
even the pit
love

Waiting for Jesus in Tucson
Hay un angel cerca de usted

behind Funeraria del Angel
ghosts ramble down the alley
stop and hover over a young woman
curled in sleep atop
a semen-blood stained mattress
they mumble among themselves
wonder about her parents
who would barely recognize
their daughter

overhead power lines stretch
from pole to pole to crosses

the ghosts want to believe
Jesus might care
but for now they perch high
dissipate in desert heat
listen for angels

Braiding His Wife's Hair

her hair just whispers now
hardly enough to braid
but he tries hard to keep the tangles
from scattering her already tired mind

sometimes she sits still
lets his fingers soothe her
he thinks she might remember
lying with him
a pine-needled floor soft
beneath them
an evergreen scent
they thought would last forever

before a storm drenched them
hard and cold
still occasional sweet dew
come morning

How To Smell Purple

on an end of February
scruffy brown snow
with only hints of green
kind of day
she stands in the post office line
waits for a package
then feels its buoyant
light-as-air box
tears it open and out spills
the smell of purple

neighbors and strangers step close
witness daphne flowers
wrapped in wet paper towels
secure in a Wonder Bread bag
and the letter signed

Love,
 Dad
P.S. Spring will come.

likely all she needs to know

Madonna Lily

grandmother of old-woman shoes and
dull flowered dresses
who are you?
hidden down steep cellar steps
leading to August in jars

but today I smell Madonna lilies
how they stood far
from peas, corn, carrots
the what's for supper night after night
for men and boys
who only grunted gratitude

but the lilies
a secret life of heady smells
maybe even erotic
only you knew
and how they might burst
in steamy Iowa heat
on a day nobody imagined

Love Beads and a Fog Horn

in that once upon a time
bell-bottoms and no bra delight
sixties
a faraway man sent letters
make love, not war
words that heated
her nights alone
in her first on her own
upstairs flat

two blocks east
Lake Michigan blew cold
the fog horn sounding wisdom
make your life count
wake up
get out of bed
dress then catch the #5 bus
punch in
wash bottoms
slide old bodies side to side
no bedsores allowed

the man from faraway cities returned
placed love beads around her neck
till one day they broke
and shattered

they grew into seeds
planted in rich dirt
hoping to be daisies
or sunflowers
blooming all over again

but quite possibly even taller

Father Bird

> "The battles of the Eastern Front (World War II) constituted the largest military confrontation in history."
>
> *The Atlantic*

maybe there really is a heaven
and we'll all meet again

a Russian woman keeps vigil
searches for her child
leery of an enemy soldier

remembers

her infant's mewling mouth
how she held him up
how the German officer
mother-birded mush to her child

the child lived
she died
he survived

now hours before his death
he wonders his life

can one kindness
wipe away a thousand regrets?

can life-death numbers
add, multiply, divide, subtract
balance the horror?

will she know him?

Oh, Darling, Stand by Me

his fingers are stubs now
and you remember
the cancer sign is a crab
and how we all lose
pieces of ourselves
but for now
you light the smoke
and your fingers become his

he inhales and exhales
waits for another breath
maybe his last

you stand by and we
(try so hard)
won't be afraid

Home Front

they wait on the porch to hear
two long one short one long
blast of whistles
the 6 a.m. train
sends her oldest off to Korea

she clutches her late in life
(breasts leaking)
child close

the little one clings tighter
their heartbeats
almost in tune
but the air is cold
and they wonder if warmth
will ever return

sixty years pass
the old woman hears
two long one short one long
whistles
stands on her porch
remembers
the click-clack
of the rails

the rhythm of their hearts

To Know Such Beauty

no longer bouncing along his hip
my father's creel sits high
now on a bookshelf
I carry it down and smell marshy grass
remember scratchy legs
slip back seventy years to Hat Creek
to cast then hold my first fish
a rainbow whose colors
carried light
her out-of-water gasps
would forever sting my ears

Last-Chance Melody

two days before he gets up
and leaves
after eighty-plus earthbound years
my grandpa tells me
get out my ol' mouth harp

it sits in a nest
of worn Kodaks
recording a now too-long life

I crank the sick bed
prop pillows
his at-one-time wife
mother of seven kin leans close
then sings old woman
cracked notes
to his wheezy, harp-tune breaths

a harmony of sorts
dances the air
hymns and tunes played back
in Depression time before
lead and zinc chewed lungs
and booze held sway

listen now
you might find yourself believing
for this little while anyway
in torn and tattered
stick around love

two doors down
Death sits patiently
hums along to a few hymns
knows not to disturb

Unnamed

when she was old
and memories were more company
than neighbors next door
and St. Mary's shadowed her window
where Father Joe
doled forgiveness
in calculated pieces
her mind wandered back
to a time
when kindness
was burying crimson sheets
and tiny remains
of creation
not meant for this world
but silenced from eyes
ready to smite
a woman certain
she must give back
to God
a life she knew
she could not hold
even as she bled
her own existence
almost away

My Mother's Temper

her voice purpled the room
no shy violet pansy
but the kind of holler
that reaches deep in your marrow
crowding blood cells
till you think
they may burst into forever
hemorrhaging wounds
and then
the tempest would pass
air now sweet and clear enough
to stitch your heart pieces
whole again

The Weight of Squid on a Full Moon Night

on Halong Bay
in the South China Sea
I bamboo jig
wait for pull and tug
the weight of squid

my pole digs deep
then leaps
a squid now flies
its shiny body lit by the moon

at lunch tomorrow
I will remember her inky eye
how it stabbed my heart
and how we fill our hunger
so dependent
on the weight of squid

Saffron Dreams

    Thousands of bloom in fall *crocus sativus*
    stigmas are used to create saffron.

two days short of November
last-hurrah leaves turning to brown
my down-the-street neighbor
surrounded by a block
of perfect green turf
has planted *crocus sativus*
extravagant purple
now in full fall glory
look again and see
yellow stamens
red-orange stigma
then learn the patience
of picking a thousand threads
but for now
before winter crashes
savor purple

Even Dead Fish Become Roses

she remembers in her last days
as cancer slips through a back door
trying to steal whatever
was good
but memories sustain her
of a time relishing
second-chance lust
even love

and how she and her man
lay on Onion River's bank
joining muck and grit
with unexpected kisses
then rolling on to the carcass
of a stinky, dead fish

an explosion of guts
and almost-pee-in-your-pants laughter
taking too many mean years
into something so sweet
even dead fish become roses
a way she learned
and would never forget
to love the flower
and the bramble

Thurston High School, 6 a.m.
twenty years after the shooting

crows crackle-caw
their early morning chatter
cruise the football field
stare down
like animated drones
they watch everything
maybe they carry
pieces of the wounded
whole souls of those lost and gone
they understand they can't change everything
but at least hope to witness
this start of day
still full of promise

Acknowledgments

Many thanks to the editors of the following publications in which these poems, sometimes in earlier versions, appeared:

Anti-Heroin Chic: "Oh, Darling, Stand by Me," "Last Chance Melody"
Bramble: "at the new big wong," "Sunflower Yellow Gem Corn Hoop Dancing"
Fox Cry: "Unnamed"
Gyroscope Review: "Transubstantiation"
Halfway Down the Stairs: "Purple Orchids and Agent Orange"
Hiroshima Day Anthology: "American Hibakusha"
MUSH: "Of Peonies and Murderous Doings"
No More Can Fit into the Evening: "Forty Years after the War"
Poetry Hall: "The Weight of Squid on a Full Moon Night," "These Feathers"
River: "Father Bird," "Hired Man Down," "Killing Field," "Uncommon Substance"
Sheltering with Poems: "Shapeshifting in Pandemic Time"
Silver Birch Press: "Last Chance Melody"
Snapdragon: Journal of Art and Healing: "My Mother's Temper"

The Water Poems: "Crossing the River at Leesburg"
Wisconsin Fellowship of Poets' Calendar: "Pang Nu Lee," "Lady
 Liberty, Mosquitoes, and Deer Flies"
Verse-Virtual: "Even Dead Fish Become Roses," "Even the
 Queen's Lace," "How Do I Write about Dragons and
 Dazzles on a Day the World Is on Fire," "Love Her Tender
 This Hard Rain Night," "Questions for the Garter Snake in
 My Backyard," "Thurston High School, 6 am," "Waiting for
 Jesus in Tucson," "Weeds"
Writing in a Woman's Voice: "Home Front," "Love Beads and a
 Fog Horn," "Smitten," "Unnamed"
Zooanthology: "Alligator Farm Blues"

The ever possibility of peonies.

Title Index

A
After the Bloom 46
Alligator Farm Blues 38
American Hibakusha 33
at the new big wong 37

B
Blue-Stemmed Goldenrod Solidago Lessons 27
Bob's Once and Forever Bomb 30
Braiding His Wife's Hair 53

C
Crossing the River at Leesburg 39

E
Even Dead Fish Become Roses 66
Even the Queen's Lace 17

F
Farm Wife Drowns 44

Father Bird 57
Forty Years After the War 29
Four-Leaf Entitlement 34

H
Hired Man Down 47
Home Front 59
Horseradish Tears 40
How Do I Write about Dazzles and Dragons
   On a Day the World Is On Fire 41
How To Smell Purple 54

I
in April 22

J
Just a Blink 50

K
Killing Field 25

L
Lady Liberty, Mosquitoes, and Deer Flies 45
Last-Chance Melody 61
Letters and Petals 48
Loss and Found 51
Love Beads and a Fog Horn 56
Love Her Tender This Hard-Rain Night 36

M
Madonna Lily 55
My Mother's Temper 63

O
Of Peonies and Murderous Doings 16
Oh, Darling, Stand by Me 58
Old Men and River Salmon 28

P
Pang Nue Le 21
Purple Orchids and Agent Orange 20
Purple-Posey Love 35

Q
Questions for the Garter Snake in My Backyard 23

R
Raspberries and Roses 26

S
Saffron Dreams 65
Shape-shifting in Pandemic Time 49
Smitten 24
Sunflower-Yellow Gem Corn Hoop Dancing 18

T
These Feathers 42
The Weight of Squid on a Full Moon Night 64
Thurston High School, 6 a.m. 67
To Know Such Beauty 60
Transubstantiation 43

U
Uncommon Substance 32
Unnamed 62

W
Waiting for Jesus in Tucson 52
Weeds 19
When We Were So Young 31

First Line Index

A
all my cousins 31
an almost lifetime ago 48
at Ben Thanh Market 20
at the farmers market 21
at thirteen 35

B
behind Funeraria del Angel 52

C
carry a big stick 45
crows crackle-caw 67

G
grandmother of old-woman shoes and 55
gulf waters cradle dolphins 38

H
her hair just whispers now 53
her voice purpled the room 63
his eyes watch over the old nurse 32
his fingers are stubs now 58

I
I chop celery, cabbage 18

if I cast a spell and say 27
in November 51
in that once upon a time 56

M

maybe there really is a heaven 57
maybe this man 40
my father is old now 28
my friend Ben 37
my grandfather tells a story 16
my mother was smitten 24
my old auntie holds out her hands 30

N

no longer bouncing along his hip 60
no longer rushing out the door 49

O

on an end of February 54
on Burnside 36
once again 25
on crimson-stained snow 50
on Halong Bay 64
on that day 43
on this August day the sky 17
out behind the lavender patch 23

S

seem innocent 42
she always knew 44
she remembers in her last days 66
sixty years after you walked 33
smell this 26
surrounded by tiny wings 41

T

the hired man lies 47
the house sinks 22
they wait on the porch to hear 59
this glorious start of day 34
too much pain 19
two days before he gets up 61
two days short of November 65

W
    when I was twelve 39
    when she was old 62

Y
    your wife taught me 46
    you work the graveyard shift 29